THE
ONE-
CALL
CL✓SE
FOR DJS

STOP CHASING PROSPECTS AND BOOK
PREMIUM CLIENTS IN ONE EASY MEETING

MARK IMPERIAL

Mark Imperial-- 1st ed.
Chief Editor, Shannon Buritz
ISBN: 978-1-954757-67-7
Remarkable Press

To DJ entertainers—the professionals who turn life's milestones into lifelong memories, and through whom I pay forward everything this industry gave me.

*And to my beautiful bride, **Shannon**—my toughest critic, sharpest editor, and the reason this book isn't twice as long.*

CONTENTS

INTRODUCTION

Why Most DJs Chase Clients (and Why You Won't Anymore)

———

"Have you ever noticed that anybody driving slower than you is an idiot, and anyone going faster than you is a maniac?"

-GEORGE CARLIN

Have you ever wondered what the *perfect* conversation would sound like if you ran into your "client soulmate?" The kind of prospect who clicks with you instantly and the whole thing feels natural, effortless, and even fun?

Before you ever learn the **3D One-Call Close Method** and the hidden psychology of why people buy, you've got to understand why selling feels hard for many DJs, and why it absolutely does not have to be that way for you.

The Real Problem Isn't Selling – It's What You Think "Selling" Is

Most DJs don't hate selling. They hate what they *think* selling is. They imagine scripts, rebuttals, and multi-step techniques. When DJs tell me they feel "weird talking about themselves," or that pitching feels like bragging, or that they don't want to sound like a commodity competing on price, I understand, because I used to do the same thing awkwardly and clumsily, with results to match.

Because everything I learned early on made selling way too complicated. Before I learned what I'm teaching you in this book, my first attempt at selling was an absolute nightmare.

My buddy in the 80s had a set of vending machines and asked if I'd help place them into local businesses. I thought:

"What's the big deal? I know the product. I'll just talk about it. Easy."

So I walk into a tire shop like I own the place, ask for the manager (something that barely works today), and shockingly, they actually get him for me.

He stands there at the counter, giving me a fair shot, and I proceed to vomit up the most confusing, rambling, five-minute pitch you've ever heard.

I talked in circles. I made zero sense. I probably looked like a guy trying to sell encyclopedias out of the trunk of his car.

After politely letting me self-destruct, the manager simply said:

"No, thank you."

That was my first taste of "selling." And it sucked.

The Rapport-Building Fiasco

I started studying sales. Books, tapes, seminars, everything. And the first big lesson I learned was to build rapport. So when I started my DJ business and got my first real cold prospect, not a friend, not family, I decided to open with what I thought was a rapport-building question.

I sat down with the couple and said:

"So... how did you two meet?"

It landed like a fart in church.

They looked at me like: *"Who ARE you and why are you asking us intimate questions?"*

Have you ever said something and immediately wished you could rewind time five seconds?

I tried to clarify, "Oh, I mean like... was it at work?" but the damage was done. They just wanted to move on, and I realized something huge in that moment:

Memorized rapport tactics ruin natural conversations.

You sound like a bad actor reading someone else's lines. Prospects today are what I call "superbugs." They're immune to old-school sales techniques. They've heard every trick.

Once they sense that you're "selling," they shut down.

Why Most DJs End Up Chasing Clients

All of this leads to the reasons most DJs struggle:

→ They're forcing sales tactics they don't believe in.
→ They rely on scripts they can't remember.
→ They try to "pitch" instead of *listen*.
→ They talk about themselves instead of discovering what the client actually wants.
→ They compete on price because they don't know how to shift the conversation.
→ They try to impress instead of understand.

And when you do that?

- Clients ghost you.
- They shop you around like a commodity.
- You feel like you're chasing when you should be attracting.

Selling Gets Easier When You Stop Selling

When you drop the scripts, the pressure, the "me-focused" pitch, and talk to clients like a collaborator rather than a salesperson, everything shifts.

People want two things:

1. To feel understood.
They want to feel *heard*. They want to feel like you get what they care about.

2. To feel certain.
They want to trust that things will be handled and that their event will turn out the way they imagine.

When you combine understanding + certainty, clients stop shopping and start choosing.

That's when selling stops feeling like selling and starts feeling like helping.

Proof It Works Even for "Non-Salespeople"

My ex-girlfriend, Christina, is a perfect example. She's a teacher with a master's degree, brilliant, but nothing like me. Totally opposite personality. She hates selling. Hates the idea of selling. Situationally shy. Not wired for persuasion at all.

When she launched her tutoring business, I helped her fill her pipeline. Seven prospects booked within 48 hours.

Her reaction was pure panic.

She said, "Mark, I can't sell! I don't want to pitch anyone!"

I told her:

"You don't have to. You only need one question and a simple conversation."

I gave her the early version of what you'll learn in the following pages, the same approach, the same structure, the same psychology, and she sold 7 out of 7 prospects, all in under an hour each.

Paid-in-full packages, too.

$550 × 7 = $3,850

In two days. With zero scripts. From someone who *hates* selling.

The beauty of it was that she barely spoke. The clients did all the talking because she created a space where they felt heard, understood, and confident.

This is the magic of the **3D One-Call Close Method**. I'll show you how to guide the prospect naturally and confidently into seeing you as the only choice with just one powerful human conversation.

The Shift Starts Here

Before we go any further, I want you to imagine an imaginary button behind your ear.

I know it sounds silly, but trust me. Picture a chalkboard filled with everything you've ever been taught or told about selling. Now take your finger, press that imaginary button, and wipe the whole thing clean.

Erase it all.

From here on out, we're starting fresh.

In the next chapter, we're diving into the hidden psychology of why people buy and refer, why this method works across every industry, and why it will work for you even if you're shy, new to sales, or allergic to anything that feels "pushy."

Once you understand *why* this works, closing becomes effortless.

KEY TAKEAWAYS

- Selling only feels hard when you're acting, posturing, or performing.

- Prospects shut down the moment they sense scripts, tactics, or anything that seems unnatural; authenticity wins every time.

- You attract clients when you stop pitching and start understanding what they want and helping them feel confident that you can deliver it.

- You don't need charisma or "sales talent"; you need the right structure that lets the client do the talking and reveals what matters most to them.

- The shift begins the moment you erase everything you thought selling was and replace it with a simple, human, one-conversation approach that makes you the obvious choice.

PART ONE

THE PSYCHOLOGY OF HIGH-CLOSING DJS

CHAPTER ONE

"How Much Do You Charge for Four Hours?"

How to Turn This Awful Question Into a Booking Once and for All

---

"Price is what you pay. Value is what you get."
-WARREN BUFFETT

You may be able to relate to this...

Your phone rings or you get an email with the most annoying question most DJs will ever get.

"How much do you charge for four hours?"

That question boils the blood of most DJs because they feel like they are starting the sales conversation on their heels. I'll show you how to handle it tactfully and turn it into a hero-sherpa conversation.

First, tell yourself that it's not their fault they're asking you this. For most people, when they don't know what they *should* be asking, often the default thought is PRICE. This is just telling you they don't know what they should be asking, and it is a signal that you can help them.

It can be a good thing that they don't know what to look for, because it lets *you* set the buying criteria! It can be a clue that they don't know what to look for or what to ask, and that gives you more control.

You won't get mad at that question anymore when you know this switch tactic. This simple reply will put you in the driver's seat...

Say this: "I'm happy to share pricing with you. Is it okay if I ask you a few questions so I can be sure I recommend the right program for you?"

Make it your own. Here's another variation: "Not a problem! I have a range of programs priced according to the type of entertainment package we create for you. Is it okay if I ask you a few questions so I can make the right recommendation?"

This response can turn your cold inbound call into a meaningful conversation, where you can choose to do the 3D One-Call Close Method. Or you can move them to an in-person meeting. Use your own judgment as to the value of the prospect and which direction is best worth your time.

My preference and first choice, whenever possible, is to switch them to a meeting, whether in person or on Zoom.

There are many nuances to this; however, I'll give you an example…

I may ask a few qualifying questions and not go into the whole 3D One-Call Close Method. I may just want to see if what they're planning is worth my time and get an idea of the budget.

After I get permission to ask them questions, I'll say, "Tell me a little bit about (your big day/what you're planning) and what you have in mind." I keep this very open to interpretation to see how they think. They may be vague or share visions of grandeur. This is valuable insight.

You may ask follow-up questions like, "Have you booked your venue yet?" or "Where are you having this?" This will give you more insights, like a budget.

After getting a clearer picture of what they want, if I deem it worth setting up a meeting, I would transition to offering an in-person or Zoom (more thorough) meeting. I would say something like, "To answer your pricing question, I have a range of programs that could work for you. Would you be open to getting together to go over some ideas in more detail?"

If they press for pricing at this early stage and only if forced, I would give them a *range*. I'd say, "The programs that sound like a good fit for you range between ($1,500 to $3,500) depending on the package you prefer. I'd also like to send you my book "Ultimate Wedding Receptions" (or my "Reception Success Kit." Are you open Friday to go over the options for your big day?"

Back in the days when we actually answered incoming phone calls, we had the task of selling over a long phone conversation. Even then, I preferred to intentionally delay gratification by setting up a meeting rather than trying to sell right then and there. Doing so would allow you to send the best pre-indoctrination materials, such as a shock-and-awe package.

Will This Work on the Phone or Zoom?

Many DJs will ask if this will work on the phone or on Zoom if they don't meet in person.

Yes, it will. I have a few things to share with you about the phone. Generations born in the late 1990s and after tend to dislike talking on the phone, preferring text and DMs instead.

Obviously, today's generation of party planners and brides will prefer brief meetings via online platforms and even keep the video off to avoid anxiety. However, the strategy and tactics remain the same.

When possible, especially if you're selling premium fee packages, shoot for in-person meetings. The second preference would be via online video, such as Zoom.

When I used to meet brides and other planners in person when I didn't have an office, I suggested meeting at their venue as the first option and at their home as a second option.

Meeting at their venue gave me other opportunities, like networking with the venue itself, where they witnessed an expert demonstration by someone who knows their stuff. Involving someone from the venue gives you a boost of rapport with them. It also allows your prospects to dream a little and visualize what you are sharing. It dispelled any skepticism about why I didn't have an office, and people came to think it's better this way.

I did have a physical office, but it was near my home, and I lived about 45 minutes from my ideal market, so it never became my showroom.

When I chose to meet at prospects' homes, there were pros and cons. The pro is that they are comfortable, and they never want to feel cheap in their own home. The major con is that they have every daily distraction around them, so I had to accept some disruption to the meeting.

So now you know that to answer that price question is not about giving a direct monetary answer, but instead to tactfully telegraph, not that they are stupid, but that there is a lot more to their question that they may not have considered, and invite them to a more in-depth and meaningful conversation. To do this, you must create a fascination so that they want to talk further with you because you have demonstrated knowledge and trust in such a short conversation. You want them to feel that meeting with you will be beneficial and fruitful for their goals.

KEY TAKEAWAYS

- When prospects lead with price, it usually means they don't yet know what they *should* be asking, which allows you to guide them.

- Ask permission to ask questions before sharing pricing so you can shift the conversation from cost to fit and value.

- Your goal is not to sell on the spot but to move the prospect into a deeper conversation where trust and understanding can be built.

- Use qualifying questions to assess vision, budget, and seriousness before deciding how much time to invest.

- Price becomes easier to discuss once you have positioned yourself as the expert and created curiosity around what is possible.

CHAPTER TWO

The Hidden Switch Inside Every Buyer's Mind

---

*"People don't buy for logical reasons.
They buy for emotional reasons."*

- ZIG ZIGLAR

If you really want to close clients easily without pushing, pitching, or feeling weird, remember this: **People don't buy because of your gear, your lighting, your mixing, your packages, or your years of experience.** They buy because of **psychology.**

I'm going to repeat something because it is that important. No matter who you're talking to, a bride, a groom, a corporate client, or a parent planning a party, every single buyer wants the **two things** we discussed in Chapter One:

1. They want to feel understood.
2. They want certainty.

When you make people feel understood AND certain, they stop shopping. They choose **you**.

People can sense immediately whether you're trying to help or trying to sell. If your energy, your frame, your vibe says "I'm here to pitch you," they tighten up. If your energy says, "I'm here to help you," they open up. It's all about how you enter the conversation.

Why Helping Works Better Than Selling

I tell every DJ: Take selling off the table. Remove it entirely. Walk into every meeting with one mission:

"I want to help this person."

And something interesting happens when you take on that frame: The right clients lean in.

And the wrong clients?

They naturally filter themselves out.

That's exactly what you want because not every client is a fit. You don't want to onboard every prospect who comes across your path. If you've ever taken on a "pain in the butt" client you wish you could fire halfway through the relationship, you know what I'm talking about.

Let me tell you what happened the night Christina had her big meeting with a tutoring prospect.

This is the same Christina I told you about earlier, the one who hates selling, is situationally shy, and doesn't have a sales bone in her body.

After she learned this method, she went into her meeting with one simple goal:

Help them.

They sat down. She asked the core question I'll teach you soon.

And then...

She barely spoke. The prospect talked. And talked. And talked. For 45 minutes, Christina mostly *listened*.

At the end of the conversation, the woman said: "Christina, you're absolutely amazing. This is going to be wonderful. I finally feel hope for my son for the first time in a long time."

Think about that: She said Christina was "amazing"…

…but Christina hardly said anything.

Christina helped her feel understood. And she helped her feel certain.

> **Helping > Selling**
> **Understanding > Pitching**
> **Listening > Talking**

This is the hidden switch inside every buyer's mind.

The Sizzle Package:
Your Pre-Indoctrination Advantage

Before we move deeper into the psychology of the meeting itself, there's a crucial piece that happens **before** the meeting even begins, and most DJs completely miss it. Once someone reaches out, whether or not you successfully schedule the meeting on that first contact, your next move is always the same:

You send your Sizzle Package.

I call it a Sizzle Package. Dan Kennedy calls it a Shock-and-Awe Package. Whatever you call it, this is your **pre-indoctrination material**, the warm-up that prepares the prospect emotionally and mentally for your conversation.

You send it **whether you got the meeting or not.**

If they agree to meet:

"Great! Let's set that up. In the meantime, I'd really love to send you my Insider Guide to Amazing Receptions." (or whatever your book or special report is called. Yes, you should create this!)

If they *don't* agree yet:

"I totally understand. Tell you what, I'd love to send you my Insider Guide to Incredible Weddings. I think it'll answer a lot of your questions, and I'll follow up with you afterward."

Either way, that package goes out because a huge part of the sale happens in the pre-indoctrination period, the window between the first contact and the actual meeting.

Most DJs wait until the meeting to begin influencing the prospect. That's a mistake.

You have a massive opportunity to set the stage early with education-based marketing. Your Sizzle Package positions you immediately as the guide who will help them. It always ends with a call to action, inviting them to speak with you. Even if they already booked the meeting, that CTA stays in there because you'll use this same package in email sequences and other outreach.

Sending your shock-and-awe package ahead of time allows your prospect to grow some "Know-(and hopefully) Like-and-Trust" toward you before your meeting. They will feel like they're talking to a celebrity!

Now, here's the mistake to avoid: Trying to accomplish too many things at once.

Don't send the Sizzle Package and then dump pricing, packages, features, and equipment. That creates clutter. This step has **one job:**

Move them to the *next* step.

For this phase, the next step is: **Get the meeting (or prepare them emotionally for the meeting you already booked).**

A quick note about qualified vs. unqualified prospects: in some industries, you must pre-screen because people want the free education but can't hire you. If you're at capacity or need to protect your time, you can put a survey or application before the meeting.

But if you're newer or have more time than money, keep the faucet open and talk to more people. Use the Sizzle Package to warm and filter naturally.

Now that you understand what happens before the meeting, let's get into the conversation itself, where the psychology really kicks in.

Framing: Your Secret Weapon

The concept of framing is something that took me years to understand fully. Framing means you:

- Know who you are in the conversation
- Know what the purpose of the conversation is
- Know what outcome you want (for *them*, not you)

Your frame is: **"I want to help you make the best possible decision for your event."**

It's powerful because people can feel your intent. They can feel if you're centered, authentic, and genuinely helpful. And they can feel if you're needy, hungry, or trying too hard. Your frame is your anchor.

If someone comes to the table with negativity, pressure, impatience, or a bad attitude, you don't try to salvage them. You simply find your own words that politely express: "You know what, I don't think we're a good match." They may ask why you have come to this conclusion. I usually don't like to explain my reasons because you might offend people, and the last thing you want is to leave a meeting with a negative feeling. You can give them a respectful response. This should not be confrontational, so you need to practice tactful ways to let them down gently.

This is very delicate, so I don't want to give you absolute advice here. Just understand the frame: You know you won't be a good fit, so you shouldn't continue in respect of both parties' time. However, you want to do this tactfully to be respectful so they don't feel slighted, and not trigger defensiveness in them. Perhaps what they said indicated they wouldn't like something you do. (Or vice versa, they may want something that you know is detrimental!) If that is the case, you may gently point it out and say, "You mentioned you didn't want the (xyz), and we find the (xyz) to be an important detail, so you may be disappointed." Stick with truthfulness and not emotion. Don't tell them their ideas are wrong. Just speak from experience. Say things like "Many people think that____but what I have found is____." Find your own words and practice them. Who knows, maybe they'll backpedal and put you back in the driver's seat. What matters is that you are transparent and you want to enjoy the events you choose to take on. People respect those who stand for something.

The ones who don't respect the process will become nightmare clients anyway.

How to Set the Frame

After the small talk is out of the way, nothing forced, nothing weird, you transition into the frame. Remember from Chapter One, don't ask, "How did you two meet?" or anything weird like that (LOL). Something like, "How's all your other planning going?" works just fine.

You say something like: "If you're open to it, I'd like to learn a little about (your day/what you're celebrating/what you're planning) so I can make the best recommendations. How does that sound?"

This does a few things:

1. **It creates safety.**
   You're signaling that this is a conversation, not a sales pitch.

2. **It removes pressure.**

   You're not launching into a monologue. You're inviting them in.

3. **It positions you as a helper, not a seller.**

4. **It puts you in control gently.**

   You're guiding the structure from the beginning.

And here's the important part: **You make zero mention of selling.** This is not where you say, "And at the end I'll show you my packages."

If they ask, "So… are you going to tell us about your pricing?" you respond: "Only if it makes sense later. For now, let's figure out what you want your day to look and feel like."

That one line dissolves pressure instantly.

Don't Skip Steps – Even When They're "Ready to Buy"

Sometimes a prospect will say: "Hey, I already know about you. I've done all my research. I just want the details on your packages."

You might think: *"Great! Slam dunk!"*

But it's not. If you skip the conversation, the discovery, the psychology, the clarity, then your offer has no context. You will be compared to every other DJ.

Never, ever skip the process.

When a prospect tries to rush you, you say: "Thanks for asking about my programs. Before I explain it, is it okay if I ask you a few questions so that I can make the right recommendation?"

That allows you to:

1. Reset the frame.
2. Get back in the driver's seat (subtly).
3. Open the door to the **3D One-Call Close** conversation.

Forget the Form

Let me save you from a mistake I've seen countless DJs make. They sit down with a prospect and pull out an official-looking form. You can almost see the client's eyes glaze over like:

"Oh great... here comes the pitch."

Forms break the natural rhythm and trigger buyer defenses immediately.

I used to use forms, and I realized they made me look canned or formulaic. It looked like a connect-the-dots. I could tell in the prospects' eyes that they were wondering, "How long is this test going to take?" LOL. It looked like I had a middle school exam to put them through.

My mentor, Dan Kennedy, pointed out, "There's no better demonstration of experience, talent, and expertise than Frank Sinatra with just a spotlight and a microphone."

If you can impromptu grab a microphone, no backup band, and perform...you're a pro.

So ever since then, instead...

I used a blank notepad.

A notepad feels safe and it signals: "I don't have a predetermined script for you. I'm here to understand you."

That builds trust faster than anything else.

Prospects Need Certainty
Before They Say Yes

Buyers today are overwhelmed by the planning for the biggest event of their lives. They are afraid of making a mistake. Fear of the unknown is the #1 driver of hesitation. This system works so well because:

- You remove fear.
- You replace it with clarity.
- You create certainty.
- You help them see their event succeed in the future.

This psychological clarity is what makes decisions easy. The more confused the mind is, the longer it takes to decide. The clearer the mind is, the faster it decides.

The next chapter reveals the Magic Question that begins the **3D One-Call Close process.**

KEY TAKEAWAYS

- People buy because they feel understood and certain, not because of your gear, résumé, or packages.

- When you walk in with the intent to help instead of sell, clients relax and often close themselves.

- The Sizzle Package warms the prospect before the meeting, making the **One-Call Close** dramatically easier.

- Framing the conversation around collaboration and clarity positions you as the trusted guide, not the pushy vendor.

- Never skip the discovery process, even with "ready to buy" prospects, or you'll get compared on price and lose your advantage.

- When you help clients organize their thoughts and calm their worries, you become the person who makes everything feel doable, and that's who buyers trust most.

PART TWO

THE 3D
ONE-CALL
CLOSE

CHAPTER THREE

The Magic Question

_____

"He that has eyes to see and ears to hear may convince himself that no mortal can keep a secret. If his lips are silent, he chatters with his fingertips; betrayal oozes out of him at every pore."

-SIGMUND FREUD

By the time you sit down with a prospect, whether it's over the phone, in your office, at their venue, or in their home, you've already done the most important work. You've framed the conversation correctly. You've taken the pressure of "selling" off the table. And you've created the kind of environment where people feel comfortable enough to be honest. Once that foundation is set, you're ready for the moment that changes the entire tone of the meeting. It's the moment where the conversation shifts from surface-level details to what truly matters.

And it all begins with a single question.

This question isn't complicated. It doesn't sound "salesy," rehearsed, or gimmicky. In fact, its simplicity is exactly what makes it so effective. It opens people up. It gets them talking, sometimes more than they've ever talked to any DJ in their whole planning process. It reveals their hopes, their concerns, and the emotional picture they already have in their minds but don't know how to express. And as you'll see, it's the key that unlocks everything else in the **3D One-Call Close system.**

At the end of the previous chapter, you got permission to move forward with the conversation. Now you need to set the ground rules! You want to do this to save time and give clarity. If you skip this step, the conversation can go wildly out of control, wander aimlessly, and waste your time! Without guidelines, the prospect can feel "uncertain" about what this conversation will be about, like walking into a room blindfolded. Remember, our whole goal is to imply "certainty" consistently. This is another subliminal feeling that gets planted. People are silently begging to be led. They won't realize or verbalize this, but for most people, if they don't have to be responsible, they gladly hand the reins over!

This is how you transition from getting permission to beginning the magic conversation.

After you ask, "If you're open to it ...", and when they say "Sure!", you say something like "Terrific! I'll ask you a few questions so I can learn about (your day/what you're celebrating/planning). Then, I can make the best recommendations for you. If "we" are a good match for you, I'll share how I can help, and you can ask any questions that come up. Sound good? (Is that cool?)." <<< I always say make these words YOUR personality.

When they say "Sounds good!" or "Yes! Let's go!", then you can get started.

How to Read Your Prospect's Mind

Before you get to the Magic Question, I'll give you my "Mind Reading Question" because it gives you tons of psychological intel right away. Before I even created my 3D One-Call Close, I used to start meetings with this, and I still include it today. Here it is...

You say, "Hey, before we dive in, if you were to describe how you want your (big day/party/whatever you're planning) to be with just three adjectives (words), what would those three words be?"

The magic in this question is that when they answer, you'll know what type of people you're dealing with. You can get a glimpse at the kind of people they are so that you can tailor your words just for them.

For example, if the three words they say are "upscale, formal, and fun," that is the opposite of "wild, crazy, and outrageous!"

One sounds stuffy and maybe even a bit boring. The other sounds like Animal House.

Can you see how hearing this upfront tells you a lot?

Whatever they say, write it down at the top of your notepad so they can see you write it! Say the words with a smile back to them as you write. "Ok! So you want it ____, ____, and ____! Got it!"

See, again, you're letting them know you're listening to them. You can be fun with them for a moment if you want, but don't overdo it. Something as simple as, "Sounds like my kind of party!" will do.

Now you can go on to the opening Magic Question...

I first learned this concept from Dan Sullivan, Founder of Strategic Coach, who specializes in helping coaches and consultants gain clients. What I did was turn it into a framework specifically for the DJ Entertainer industry.

Here is the magic opening question...

> **I'll start by asking...** *"If we were having this conversation a few weeks after your (big day/celebration, or whatever it is), and you were looking back, what has to have happened for you to feel the happiest about how everything turned out?"*

There is a lot of MAGIC that happens with that question! (Translation: a lot of psychology happens in your prospect's mind!)

When you ask this question, something fascinating happens. Instead of thinking like shoppers comparing DJs, packages, and prices, your prospects immediately slip into *vision mode* by doing the following:

1. It future-paces them.

They begin imagining themselves in the future, after the event is over, looking back at everything that happened. It moves them past their current stress and uncertainty and places them in a mental space where everything has gone well.

2. It removes current pain.

As soon as they picture the future, their present stress disappears long enough for them to speak openly.

3. It triggers the "Theater of the Mind."

People cannot help but visualize their event when you frame it this way. They picture the room, the people, the music, the atmosphere, the emotions, and the overall experience they hope to create. In doing so, they begin describing the exact details you need to guide the conversation, deepen the relationship, and eventually make a recommendation that feels perfectly aligned with their vision.

4. It gets them talking (hopefully, a lot).

The key here is to ask the question naturally and then say nothing. Most DJs rush to fill the silence because they're used to performing or providing information. But here, silence is your friend. When you give people space, they fill it, and often, they fill it with gold. Some folks may be brief, while others may talk for many uninterrupted minutes. They may describe what they fear, what they're excited about, what they hope guests will feel, and what would make the day truly special for them. And because you're not selling, they don't feel guarded. They feel heard.

They may talk too much! That can be okay, as long as you want to listen. However, if the conversation takes a negative turn, you must reel them back in. For example, if your prospect has felt any struggle or pain in planning this event, you don't want them to sit in their pain. You want to show them the light. This is rare, and I have encountered it only once or twice in my career. I had a Debbie-Downer type client who only talked badly about every vendor they met, every venue they saw, and every option they were presented with.

I reeled them back in by saying, "Wow, that must feel frustrating! Let's talk about what would have to happen for you to be happy!" Then we continued the conversation in a positive direction. I left this part out, but this is what I was implying: ("Hey, we can waste all day talking about what you hate and what got you here, or we can talk about solutions to get you out of that pain!") Remember, I didn't say that! But, I was thinking it to myself!

5. It makes you the most helpful person they've spoken to.

Other DJs talk about gear. You talk about *their lives.*

From experience, prospects fall into three categories:

1. **The Ones Who Immediately Jump In**

    They say, "That's a great question," and begin sharing everything. This is a great sign! These are the people you will love and want to work with the most.

2. **The Ones Who Want to Answer But Don't Know How**

    You'll see long pauses. They struggle to articulate. These folks often need a little nudge, like: "Some couples tell me they worry about people not dancing or the music not being right, but every event is different. What comes to mind for you?" They'll open up after that. These can be wonderful clients; they just need a guide.

3. **The Ones Who Won't Play**

    If someone says: "Um, I don't see the point of this. Can you just tell me your prices?" That's a red flag. You can help the willing. You can never help someone who refuses the process. When someone is closed off from the start, they will be closed off for the entire relationship. And it is *always* better to walk away early than suffer through months of headaches.

What You Do While They Talk

As they talk, your job is simple: listen actively and take notes on a blank notepad. A plain sheet of paper signals that this is a genuine conversation, not a predetermined questionnaire. While they're speaking, nod, react naturally, and jot down the points that matter. Active listening doesn't involve repeating words back like a robot. Make them feel understood through your presence, your attention, and the moments where you acknowledge their feelings with a genuine, "I hear you," or "That makes sense." A nuance to that are expressions like, "I can see that!" or "Looks good to me!" Visual people use terms related to vision, like "I see." Auditory people will say things like, "Sounds good!" This isn't a big thing, but if you can pick up on these clues, you can mirror them by using "hear" or "see" terms accordingly.

As you listen, you'll learn:

- ★ Their biggest fears
- ★ Their expectations
- ★ What a "perfect" day means to them
- ★ What they don't want to happen

★ What they absolutely DO want to happen
★ Their emotional priorities
★ What motivates their decisions

This is the information that every DJ *wishes* they had, but most never get. You get it in the first ten minutes.

And best of all, you didn't have to sell, pitch, or prove anything.

KEY TAKEAWAYS

- Once you set the tone of certainty and leadership, the entire conversation becomes easier because the prospect feels guided instead of pressured.

- The Magic Question instantly shifts people out of "shopping mode" and into vision mode, where they open up, future-pace themselves, and tell you exactly what matters most to them.

- Silence after the question is your superpower. When you stop talking, they start revealing gold you could never pull out with scripts or sales tricks.

- Their response tells you everything: the open ones are ideal, the hesitant ones need gentle guidance, and the closed-off ones will always be a headache.

- When you listen actively, take notes, and genuinely care, you become the most helpful person they've spoken to without selling, pitching, or trying to prove yourself.

CHAPTER FOUR

D1: Dangers

"Avoiding danger is no safer in the long run than outright exposure."

-HELEN KELLER

Everything you uncovered in the "Magic Question" conversation naturally leads into the next part of the process, the **3D Method**:

1. **Dangers**
2. **Dreams**
3. **Dependables**

These three dimensions deepen the conversation and give you even clearer insight into what your prospect values most. Now it's time to explore the first **"D"** of the **3D Method: Dangers**, the risks, fears, and concerns they carry with them, often silently.

Most DJs never realize that people buy solutions to escape pain faster than they buy to gain pleasure. When a prospect is worried about something going wrong, they're far more motivated to take action than when they're just thinking about "nice-to-have" features.

But unlike high-pressure sales techniques that dwell on fear, you aren't manufacturing anxiety. The goal is to understand the fears they already have, and show them they're safe with you.

The Dangers Question

Once the Magic Question is fully answered, you transition with:

> *"If we were having this conversation a few weeks after your (big day/celebration, or whatever it is), and you were looking back over those months of planning, what dangers would you have had to have avoided or overcome for you to feel thrilled about it?"*

Just like the Magic Question, this one shifts the focus, but this time toward what they hope to avoid. Look at it as grounding rather than negative. Every event has risks. Every couple, every client, has concerns. When you ask this question, you create a safe space for them to say out loud what they've probably been worrying about internally. The psychology behind **Dangers** is simple but powerful:

❖ **People fear pain more than they pursue pleasure.**
   If they imagine something going wrong, it creates urgency, clarity, and honesty.

❖ **Naming the fear reduces the fear.**
   Once the danger is spoken out loud, it becomes a problem they can solve instead of something silently eating at them.

❖ **You become the DJ who actually understands their world.**
   When you address their fears with empathy instead of dismissing them, you instantly stand apart from everyone else.

❖ **You discover the real reasons they buy.**
   Some of the most common dangers prospects will share with you when you give them the chance are:

   • "I'm scared people won't dance."
   • "I'm afraid the music won't match our style."

- "What if the DJ doesn't listen to us?"
- "What if something goes wrong with the timeline?"
- "What if no one has fun?"
- "What if the MCing feels cheesy or cringey?"
- "What if people don't like the vibe or theme we chose?"

These are emotional dangers and the absolute best drivers of decisions.

How to Handle Clients Who Struggle to Answer

Not everyone will know what to say right away. Some prospects have never been asked to think this way. If they pause or look unsure, you can gently guide them.

A simple prompt works:

"Some couples tell me they worry about people not dancing, or the music not fitting their crowd. What concerns come to mind for you?"

You're merely giving them an example. This unlocks the conversation without leading them or putting words in their mouth. You're permitting them to articulate what's already there.

And if you run into those people who absolutely don't want to "play" or collaborate, it's perfectly fine to switch the conversation to, "I don't think we're a good match, but I can recommend a few DJs who might be a better fit."

Remember: The One-Call Close doesn't work on everyone. It works on the right people. And the right people *want* to tell you what they're afraid of.

Prioritizing Dangers

Once the prospect reveals their dangers, you don't correct them or counter them. You simply:

1. Take notes.
Write their fears down exactly as they say them.

2. Repeat the top ones back to them.
Not all of them, just the meaningful ones. This shows you were listening.

3. Ask them to choose their top three.
If they give you a long list of dangers, this is deliberate. People often list many dangers, but only a few truly matter.

Prioritizing forces clarity and gives you deep insight into what they care about most. When you do this, you help them focus, and they feel more certain about the rest of the conversation.

Now that you've learned the dangers, the fears, and the risks your prospects want to avoid, you've opened the door to the next dimension: **Dreams.** Dangers tell you what they want to escape. Dreams tell you what they want to achieve.

Together, they create the emotional contrast that makes your offer feel inevitable.

In the next chapter, we'll talk about how to bring their dreams to life vividly, emotionally, and in a way that makes you the DJ who "gets them" better than anyone else.

KEY TAKEAWAYS

- People buy faster to avoid pain than to gain pleasure, so uncovering dangers gives you the clearest insight into what truly drives their decisions.

- When you ask prospects to name their fears, you give them relief, clarity, and a safe place to say what's been worrying them.

- Writing down their dangers, repeating the meaningful ones, and asking them to choose their top three builds trust and sharpens the rest of the conversation.

- You're never manufacturing fear; you're revealing what's already there and showing them they're safe with you.

- Once dangers are revealed, you create the emotional contrast that sets up the next step: moving from what they want to avoid to the dreams they want to achieve.

CHAPTER FIVE

D2: Dreams

_____

*"All our dreams can come true if we
have the courage to pursue them."*

-WALT DISNEY

The next step is to shift the emotional energy of the conversation. You've acknowledged what your prospect wants to avoid. Now it's time to discover what they *want to create*. This is where it gets exciting, because people don't only buy to escape pain, they also buy to move toward pleasure. The **Dreams** conversation taps into the emotional core of what they're hoping their big day will feel like. And when people start talking about what they *want*, they become animated, expressive, and engaged. You'll see smiles, laughter, and enthusiasm. Their energy changes completely.

That shift is exactly what you want.

Dangers expose the emotional stakes. Dreams reveal the emotional reward.

Together, they give you everything you need to guide them effortlessly toward a confident decision.

The Dreams Question

To ask this question, keep the same structure you used before and change the focus:

> *"If we were having this conversation a few weeks after your (big day/celebration, or whatever it is), and you were looking back over those months of planning, what dreams would you have had to capture for you to feel thrilled about it?"*

The familiarity of this question puts them at ease, and the word "dreams" sparks imagination.

Just like before, ask the question and let them talk.

Their answers will tell you:

- What they hope their guests feel
- The moments they're excited about
- The kind of atmosphere they want
- The emotional tone they're imagining
- The highlights they're secretly hoping for
- The memories they want to make or relive
- The parts of the night that matter most to them

When people talk about their dreams, they open up in a different way. You'll see their eyes light up. You'll hear their voices change. They'll start describing the parts of the event that have meaning to them. This is theater of the mind in action.

Why Dreams Are So Powerful

When your prospect starts imagining their event at its absolute best, several important things happen psychologically:

- **They enter the emotional experience they want to buy.**
  You're no longer discussing logistics, you're shaping a feeling. That's what clients really hire you for.

- **They picture you as the guide who can make it happen.**
  The more clearly they can articulate their dream, the more clearly they can imagine you helping bring it to life.

- **They reveal what they truly value.**
  Some clients want elegance. Others want energy. Some want a packed dance floor. Others want a stress-free experience. Dreams tell you their emotional hierarchy.

- **They design their own buying criteria.**
  They're literally telling you the reasons they'll choose you.

What Clients Will Tell You in Their Dreams

This part of the conversation feels like you're painting a picture together. Here are the kinds of things you'll hear:

- "I want the dance floor packed all night."
- "We want a fun, classy vibe, not cheesy."
- "I want our first dance to feel magical."
- "I want our families to feel connected."

- "We want people saying it was the best wedding they've been to."
- "I want everything to feel smooth and easy."

Notice how personal these are.

They're not saying:

- "I want 12 uplights."
- "I want a specific brand of speaker."

They're saying what they want to *feel*. And when people speak from emotion, the close becomes effortless.

Your Role During This Part of the Conversation

Dreams create a natural opportunity for connection, creativity, and collaboration. Lean in by sharing ideas that add to their vision.

You might say things like:

- "You know what might be cool…"
- "I've seen this done before and it was incredible…"
- "There's a moment we can build here that your guests will love…"

As you do, take notes, just like before. And when they've expressed everything that matters, summarize their main dreams back to them and ask them to choose their top three. This forces clarity, and it tells you what to focus on later when you finally recommend your program.

Most DJs never hear any of this because they never ask. They jump straight into packages and pricing, which completely misses the emotional center of the sale. By contrast, you're discovering what they feel in their gut, what they want more than anything else.

Read back to them their top three dreams and reiterate, with a smile, why they chose those three. Again, this gets them visualizing those dream items.

When you eventually say: "Based on everything you told me, here's what I recommend..."

It feels like alignment, like you're helping them achieve exactly what they told you they wanted. You are guiding instead of selling. They want their dreams brought to life. You're proving to be the one who understands them well enough to do it.

KEY TAKEAWAYS

- Dreams shift the conversation from avoiding pain to creating excitement, while clients imagine their event at its absolute best.

- When people describe their dreams, they reveal what they truly value, including the feelings, moments, and atmosphere they want you to create.

- Their emotional vision becomes their buying criteria, making the close feel natural instead of forced.

- Your role is to lean in, collaborate, and add ideas that elevate their vision by taking notes and helping them clarify what matters most.

- When you later make your recommendation, it feels like alignment. You're giving them exactly what they told you they wanted.

CHAPTER SIX

D3: Dependables

"Trust men, and they will be true to you; treat them greatly, and they will show themselves great."

-RALPH WALDO EMERSON

By the time you reach the final dimension of the **3D Method**, **Dependables**, your prospects have already shared a lot with you. They've opened up about their fears and the things they absolutely don't want happening on their big day. They've described their dreams, the emotional high points they want to experience, and the vision they're excited to bring to life.

At this stage of the conversation, something important is already happening beneath the surface. They're starting to trust you. They're beginning to feel like you get them. And now, with one more simple question, you're going to help them tie it all together in a way that gives them even more clarity and confidence.

Dependables is the part of the method that almost no other DJ, salesperson, planner, or consultant ever touches. Yet it's one of the most influential parts of the conversation because it taps into something deep: people want to know that they're not doing this alone. They want to feel supported. They want to feel like the people around them and the structure around the event will help everything come together. So you guide them to identify the relationships, resources, and emotional anchors they can count on.

The Dependables Question

Just like the previous steps, this transition is smooth and feels natural. You continue the same future-paced framing and ask:

> *"If we were having this conversation a few weeks after your (big day/celebration, or whatever it is), and you were looking back over those months of planning, who and what would you have relied on that helped make everything go smoothly?"*

Some people will answer quickly and confidently, while others will pause and reflect. Either response is perfect. You're not looking for any specific answer. You're observing how they think about the people in their world.

When clients begin talking about who they can depend on, they reveal a tremendous amount about their emotional landscape. You'll hear about the people who calm them down, the friends who step up, the family members who mean the most to them, and the relationships that bring comfort and stability. Some will talk about parents. Some will talk about siblings. Some will talk about friends, mentors, and coworkers.

And some will say, "Honestly, we don't have a lot of people to depend on… which is why we're being careful about who we bring into this."

That last one is powerful. It means they will place a high value on your reliability.

In every case, you're uncovering who matters to them and why. You're learning the support structures that will influence their planning decisions and tapping into the emotional roots of why this event matters. And most importantly, you're guiding them toward a sense of stability and confidence about the event.

Why Dependables Make Clients Feel Safe with You

There's a reason this step seals the close. When people talk about their **Dangers** (what they fear) and then their **Dreams** (what they want), they create emotional contrast. But when they talk about their **Dependables**, they create emotional grounding. They reconnect to the people they love and the support they believe in. It stabilizes their thinking, calms any lingering anxiety, and makes them feel hopeful and capable.

You become part of that emotional grounding. You become one of the people they can rely on.

You're no longer "the DJ." You're someone who understands their relationships and fits into the emotional foundation of their event. Many DJs never create this level of trust or depth in a conversation, so they struggle with objections, ghosting, and indecision. You won't experience that.

How to Use What They Share

As they talk, take notes just as you have throughout the process. Write down the names of important people, relationship dynamics, and stories. Once they finish, you summarize their **Dependables** back to them, along with the **Dangers** and **Dreams** they previously shared. This completes the emotional arc. They see their fears acknowledged, their dreams understood, and their support system mapped out. They feel fully seen and safe enough to book with you.

Where This Leads Next

Now you have everything you need to make a recommendation that feels personalized, relevant, and deeply aligned with their emotional picture. The **Dangers** show you what they want to avoid. The **Dreams** show you what they want to achieve. The **Dependables** show you who they care about and what they rely on.

When you eventually present your solution, it will feel like the next obvious step. There's no pressure. There's no persuasion. There's no hard close. It's just a natural continuation of the clarity you've already helped them create.

In the next chapter, you'll learn how to transition from the **3D Method** into your offer using the same calm, conversational tone you've used throughout the process.

KEY TAKEAWAYS

- By the time you reach **Dependables**, the prospect already feels understood. This final question deepens that trust by revealing who and what emotionally grounds them.

- When clients talk about the people they rely on, they naturally calm down and feel more confident about their decisions.

- Their answers show you the emotional support structure around their event, including the level of reliability and stability they expect from you.

- Summarizing their **Dangers**, **Dreams**, and **Dependables** back to them completes the emotional arc and makes booking with you feel safe and obvious.

- When you transition to your recommendation, it will feel like the natural next step in the clarity you've already created together.

PART THREE
CLOSING TIME

CHAPTER SEVEN

The Close: How to Ask for the Sale Without Ever "Selling"

———

"The only way I can get you to do anything is by giving you what you want."

-DALE CARNEGIE

Now we're going into the part everyone thinks is the "hard" part. The good news is, this should be the easiest part of the entire process if you've done everything right. It feels more like a natural next step than an actual "close."

Here's exactly what I do before I ask for the sale.

I recap what we talked about, reassuring them that their ideas were great.

I'll say things like:

"Hey, that was awesome, you talking about how you grew up in the 80s… that was such a fun era… and that medley you talked about having? That sounds fantastic."

Notice what I *didn't* say:

I didn't say I was making the medley. I didn't say I was promising it. I didn't say I was including it. I only provided reassurance that their ideas were great.

Then I revisit the top two or three priorities in each area, the things that are clearly on their mind, the things that matter most.

Next, I highlight some ideas I gave them throughout the conversation. Something like:

"That medley would be so cool if, when they played it, the people who used to do that dance with you at work came out and led it for everyone."

This is important. You're showing them that you listened, that you remembered, and that you've already begun mentally designing their experience.

The Easiest Ask in the World

Now here comes the ask, and it's so simple it almost feels wrong. After the recap, I ask them:

"Does that sound like a party?"

Then:

"How do you feel about that?"

If you've done this right, they're going to feel freakin' awesome. Why wouldn't they? Most of the conversation came from *them*. You took them by the hand and guided them on an adventure they've never taken before, walking them through their own dreams, their own expectations, their own emotional picture.

People are silently begging to be led. So when you ask, "How do you feel about that?" the answer is almost always:

"It feels amazing."

"It sounds perfect."

"That feels right."

And that sets up the super hard close. Brace yourself. Here it is:

"Would you like my help?"

That's it.

Or:

"How'd you like my help creating this?"

That's the whole thing.

When you ask that question, you're not "closing" them. You're asking for the invitation to share how you help. Notice that you've delayed any selling throughout the whole conversation (packages, equipment, and features were never discussed) and focused on *vision* and *value*.

Most prospects have NEVER experienced anything like that. So this is where you wait for that enthusiastic invitation:

"Yes..."

"What does that look like?"

"Where do we start?"

That's when you say:

"Thank you for inviting me to explain my program."

This line reinforces that you weren't trying to sell them. *They invited YOU. They gave YOU permission.* And now you're simply honoring their request.

Important Notes About Assuring the Deal

Everyone has their own way of onboarding clients and presenting their program. I'm not here to change what already works for you. But here are the critical points you MUST understand to assure the deal, especially on the spot.

1. Less is more. <<<< This is the #1 takeaway in this whole book!

I don't care how many programs you have or how many options you offer; this is NOT the time to dump everything on them. This is where most entertainers blow the deal. This is what I've watched create tons of "think-it-overs." This is EXACTLY what causes DJs to have to play "chase" and lose tons of deals. You're not trying to accomplish a hundred things here. You're trying to achieve one: Agreement that YOU are the person they want to work with.

2. Do NOT dump packages.

Don't list the singers, dancers, horn sections, and uplights. If you overwhelm them, the sale dies. A confused mind makes no decision. Think of a restaurant menu. Too many choices? People freeze.

3. Focus the sale on the REAL priority: Reserving their date.

Dates are your inventory. Entertainment is one of the rare industries with built-in scarcity, real scarcity, not the fake kind marketers try to conjure up. For consultants or advisors, scarcity stems from capacity constraints. You can only serve so many clients. For DJs, scarcity comes from the date. So the focus is: "The most important thing right now is simply knowing if I'm the person you want to work with. If so, let's reserve your spot."

4. Use a retainer.

In my entertainment business, my retainers ranged from $500 to $1,000, with most at $1,000. I make them make the bigger decision later. You're not asking them to choose the package, design, add-ons, and enhancements right now. You're asking for ONE decision: "Do you want to work with me?"

And if the answer is yes, you get the retainer.

The Magic "Mechanism" That Avoids "Think-It-Overs"

You've demonstrated that you're the obvious expert they want to work with. You've let them know that they don't need to make any big decisions now, but merely to know with confidence that you're the one they want to work with, almost for sure.

So, how do you make them feel comfortable enough to retain you? You make it risk-free.

As far as I know, I'm the first person to have invented the **fully refundable, no-risk retainer.**

The gist is that I give them 10 days to change their mind or meet with other vendors.

I tell them there's no risk to lock your date on my calendar now, and you still have 10 days if you're unsure or want to meet with anyone else. If, for any reason, you choose to go with anyone else during those 10 days, simply let me know, and you'll never be charged.

By removing the risk entirely, you're giving them the ultimate comfort they need to say yes. With a couple, I have found they don't even need to talk privately to make this decision. Often, they look at each other and nod before telling me, "Yes, let's do it."

Over many years and hundreds of events, I have had only one couple take me up on that retainer refund, and it was only because they were gifted another specific entertainer for their wedding.

We could speculate on why this works so well, and my ego would tell me that they've made a wise decision because they are so smart. LOL. However, in my observation, people would rather check something off the list than keep it open. They only have about a million other things to tend to, so I feel that once they are confident they have done their due diligence and made a wise choice, they want to check it off their list and move on.

What About Pricing?

Of course, price is a concern for people, but it should NOT be the primary concern right now.

Here's what I do:

If I have three packages, I show them the range, but I do NOT go into depth: No itemized lists.

No "you get 6 of these, 12 of these." Just enough to show them the sizzle, not the details. This signals confidence: "I've got the goods. You don't need to decide any of that right now. There's plenty of time for that."

And then:

I get the retainer.

The #1 deal killer in entertainment is forcing a package decision too early. Get the main decision out of the way first: **Do you want to work with me?** Save the rest for later as part of the onboarding experience, which can actually be FUN for them.

That's how you close without ever "closing."

The Magic Behind the Method

When you lead people through their own **Dangers**, **Dreams**, and **Dependables,** you become more than a DJ. You become the person who brought clarity to the biggest moment of their lives. That's why this **1-Call Close** works. When you show up like that, clients don't have to be convinced. They invite you in. They choose you with confidence. And they tell everyone they know about the DJ who made everything feel easy. You now have the blueprint.

You now have the psychology. And you now have a way of selling that never feels like selling. Lead your prospects, elevate your conversations, and create certainty. If you do that, you'll never chase another client again because the right clients will always find their way to you.

KEY TAKEAWAYS

- Recap your prospect's ideas and priorities in a natural way that reassures them you listened, without promising anything you didn't offer.

- Ask the most disarming question in sales, "Would you like my help?" and let them invite you to share how you work.

- Keep the offer simple: no package dumping, no long menus, no overwhelm, just clarity that you're the person they want.

- Focus on the real priority: reserving the date with a straightforward retainer instead of forcing big decisions too early.

- Lead them through Dangers, Dreams, and Dependables, and they'll choose you with confidence without you ever needing to "sell."

CHAPTER EIGHT

FAQ: Additional Considerations When Selling

"Successful people ask better questions, and as a result, they get better answers."

-TONY ROBBINS

Q: Does the 3D conversation work over the phone, or only face-to-face?

A: Absolutely! It works in both settings. I've always preferred face-to-face for DJ entertainment, but I sell all my consulting over the phone using this same process. The only difference: I _schedule_ the call instead of running the full conversation the moment a cold inquiry comes in.

Q: What if I'm competing with preferred-vendor lists or clients seeing multiple DJs?

A: Focus on being your best, ideal self. When you lead prospects through a conversation they've never experienced anywhere else, you automatically rise above comparison. Competitors are talking features. You're talking transformation. And when you get that retainer, give them a few "safety-net" days to cancel if they truly want to. Most don't. They talk it over and decide, "Forget it, let's just book you."

Q: What if the clients have no vision? They say, "I have no idea what I want."

A: Sometimes they don't understand the question. Other times, they're so overwhelmed or so stressed that they can't see past the pain. Those clients tend to be difficult at every stage of planning. If they're confused, guide them. If they're combative or shut down, that's a sign they may not be your ideal client, and it's perfectly fine to move on.

Q: What about competing on price? What if someone else is charging half as much as I do?

A: I don't play the price game, ever. My go-to line: "I can't economically do that." It communicates confidence, boundaries, and that you actually know your numbers. And remember: your best clients aren't buying speakers, lights, or lists of features. They're buying *you*, the experience, the confidence, and the emotional transformation you create. When you sell value, not stuff, you take yourself out of comparison entirely.

Q: How do I get more meetings? People won't answer emails or return calls.

A: Your challenge isn't closing; you're great once you're in front of them. Your challenge is converting suspects into prospects. Don't answer price-shopping emails with prices. Answer with permission-based pivots:

"I've got a range of programs depending on your dream. Is it okay if I learn about your day so I can recommend the right one?"

Or begin with a takeaway:

"I'm not sure yet if I'm the right fit. Can I ask you a couple of quick questions first?"

You're simply trying to get the conversation because that's where you win.

Q: Is there anything else DJs should know that wasn't yet covered or asked?

A: According to author Marcus Sheridan, today 80% of decisions are made <u>before</u> ever calling a vendor! In the old days, people would usually call vendors <u>first</u> because they had all the information and answers. Today, everything you want to know is already online in the form of content marketing. YOU better be the one giving this information. Whether it's on your YouTube channel, a podcast, or merely a blog section of your website, you need to play ball with content marketing. This is a big, fluid topic for another book that I'm writing. However, I can summarize it here: You're essentially going to be expanding your shock-and-awe package; your pre-indoctrination material. You'll be breaking down that information, adding more in bite-sized chunks, and making it public. You should start by answering frequently asked questions, because if they are frequently asked, they are frequently searched. You want your videos to pop up as the answers to those questions.

EPILOGUE

*"Absorb what is useful, discard what is useless,
and add what is specifically your own."*
-BRUCE LEE

If you've read this far and did not skip ahead, that tells me something important. You were genuinely interested in this topic. More than likely, you have been browbeaten by prospects asking, "How much do you charge for four hours?" You may have spent weeks or even months chasing brides and other prospects, following up endlessly, only to end up empty-handed.

So first, congratulations. You made it to the end. More importantly, you now have everything you need to change that situation once and for all.

You no longer have to live as a commodity. You no longer have to be ping-ponged around by price shoppers and cheapskates. You now understand what it takes to become a value-driven leader. You know how to demonstrate your experience and expertise without being salesy. You understand the strategies, tricks, and tactics that allow you to sell a client in one sitting, with confidence and clarity.

Now comes the moment of truth.

You have a simple choice to make.

You can keep doing what you have always done and keep getting what you have always gotten. Prospects that never close. Prospects who choose your competition because they do not know the criteria they should be following. Or you can commit to trying something that has been proven over hundreds of my own clients and thousands of my students' clients.

Money loves speed and action. The time to ask for the retainer is at the height of emotion, not weeks or months later when the excitement has faded, and your experience has been forgotten.

If you liked what you learned here and want more curated best practices from a community of ambitious, forward-thinking professionals who believe in collaboration because rising tides raise all ships, I invite you to take the next step. I lead this community, someone whose entire career has depended on acquiring clients and who has seen just about everything there is to see in this business. That next step is joining our movement, our community, our association, the DJ Entertainers Association, which you'll read about in the next chapter.

Here is how to get started.

First, take advantage and join DJEA today for $1. For one dollar, you gain access to foundational marketing and sales trainings that have been honed over decades of experience in the DJ entertainment business. Second, join the conversation with a curated community of ambitious DJ entertainer professionals and avoid the questionable characters and dicey advice found in free online groups and forums. Third, participate in our Mastermind calls to ask the most pressing questions of the day and stay on top of the latest discoveries in service, marketing, and sales as they happen.

It is only one dollar. If you do not think it is the most incredible community and resource for growing your business, there is no risk, as that dollar is refundable. After the trial, your membership can continue at the lowest dues ever seen for an association at this level.

As you continue to grow, remember this. Do not play the hero. Play the guide. Let your clients be the hero in their own celebration. Everyone loves the guide, whether it is Obi-Wan Kenobi or Yoda. And everyone wants a guide who has a solid plan. When you adopt this framework into your blood, prospects and clients will see you as the obvious expert guide they want to work with. As that position becomes clear, your reputation will solidify. Word on the street will spread. Your business will grow.

If you give value ten times, even one hundred times, what you ask for in return, would you agree that the world becomes a better place? Go forth and spread your talents and gifts. Help more people celebrate the milestones in their lives. Maximize their magic moments. Create golden memories that will last a lifetime.

–Mark Imperial

Raising How DJs Are Seen.
Raising What DJs Are Worth.

ABOUT THE DJ ENTERTAINERS ASSOCIATION (DJEA)

What an Association Was Always Meant to Be

―――

"When professionals stand alone, nothing changes. When they stand together, they shape the market."

-MARK IMPERIAL

If this book changed how you think about sales, pricing, or the conversations you have with prospective clients, it didn't happen by accident.

The ideas in these pages were developed through years of working with professional DJs who care deeply about standards, clarity, and doing this work at a higher level. They were pressure-tested in honest conversations, refined through real wins and losses, and shaped inside a professional community that understands one simple truth:

How DJs are seen will always determine what DJs are worth.

That work lives inside the DJ Entertainers Association.

The Real Problem DJs Face

Most DJs are underpaid because the market cannot distinguish between a professional and a commodity.

Without a clear standard, every DJ looks the same.

When every DJ looks the same, clients default to price.

When price becomes the comparison, everyone loses.

This is not a talent gap.

It is a positioning gap.

And it is exactly why DJEA exists.

Better Clients Are Already Out There

Some clients value professionalism.

Some clients care about experience, leadership, and certainty.

Some clients are willing to pay for quality.

But those clients need signals.

They need standards.

They need clarity.

When the bar is invisible, they guess.

When the bar is clear, they choose differently.

Raise the bar, and the conversation changes.

The Role DJEA Was Built to Play

An association was never meant to be a noisy forum or a logo you pay for once a year.

At its best, an association provides three things:

- A curated community of professionals who take the work seriously.
- Best practices and tools that remove guesswork and elevate performance.
- Standards that the market can recognize and trust, promoted to the market.

That is what DJEA was created to be.

DJEA is a professional home for DJs who refuse to compete on price and prefer to compete on clarity, confidence, and standards.

It is also the home of the Entertainment Service Excellence (ESE) Standard.

Why Experience Matters More Than Explanation

The fastest way to understand the value of DJEA is to experience the community, the standards, and the systems firsthand.

The DJEA is intentionally structured to let you step inside before making a long-term decision.

You are given access.

You are given tools.

You are given context.

Then you decide.

What You Get Inside DJEA

When you join DJEA, you are stepping into a professional ecosystem built to elevate how DJs are seen and how they sell.

That includes proven frameworks for handling the most damaging sales conversations DJs face, complete systems for positioning yourself as a professional instead of a commodity, live guidance that replaces guesswork with clarity, and direct feedback designed to sharpen how you present yourself to the market.

Over $2,800 in professional DJ training, systems, and resources. Included when you join DJEA for $1.

NEW BOOK: The One-Call Close for DJs
Paperback book by Mark Imperial
Turn "How much do you charge for four hours?" into a booking in one easy meeting.
Value: $19

The One-Call Close for DJs – The Full Workshop
Complete sales system on video.
Close premium clients in one conversation.
Value: $197

The Original DJ's Edge Marketing System
The exact positioning system used by DJs who built six- and seven-figure businesses.
Classic, timeless, foundational.
Originally sold for $1,497

Weekly "I Love Mondays" Mastermind Calls
Live guidance, clarity, and accountability. Fun!
Value: $200

Brand & Marketing Audit (First 100 Founding Members)
Submit one piece for direct professional feedback.
Value: $900

TOTAL REAL-WORLD VALUE

Over $2,800

The Future of DJEA

DJEA is building the infrastructure that strengthens DJs individually and advances the profession collectively. Core member benefits will include:

- **MARKETING:** Ready-to-use materials for DJs
- **SOFTWARE:** Integrated booking, CRM, email, video, and SMS communication built for real DJ businesses
- **CERTIFICATION:** Display verified professional standards that instantly build trust
- **INSURANCE:** Access DJ business and event-specific insurance coverage
- **MEMBER BENEFITS:** Preferred pricing on vehicle rentals, hotels, and essential business services
- **DJEA market-facing campaigns:** Branding, marketing, and advertising that reshape public perception and elevate the value of professional DJs
- And more to come

Why This Invitation Exists

DJEA exists because DJs were never meant to do this alone.

When professionals stand together, standards rise.
When standards rise, perception changes.
When perception changes, value follows.

If this book resonated with you, DJEA is where this work continues.

JOIN DJEA FOR $1

Experience everything. Decide with confidence.

Begin with $1. Continue only if DJEA earns its place at the lowest current member rate available.

If one idea you take from DJEA leads to one booking you would not have made otherwise, the economics speak for themselves.

DJEntertainersAssociation.org

ABOUT MARK IMPERIAL

Mark Imperial is a DJ industry veteran, sales strategist, and community builder who has spent decades helping professional DJs stop competing on price and start leading conversations with confidence.

After building and running a successful DJ entertainment company himself, Mark saw a problem that never seemed to go away. Talented, hardworking DJs were being treated like commodities, not because they lacked skill, but because the industry lacked clear standards, shared language, and a better way to sell what professionalism actually means.

Rather than chasing trends or gimmicks, Mark focused on something more fundamental: how DJs communicate value.

That work led to the creation of The One-Call Close, a sales framework designed specifically for professional DJs who want to book better clients without pressure, scripts, or endless follow-up. The method teaches DJs how to take control of the conversation, establish buying criteria, and lead prospects to a confident decision in a single meeting.

Mark is the author of *The Ultimate Wedding Reception*, *Remarkable Receptions*, the original *DJ's Edge Marketing System*, and founder of the DJ Entertainers Association (DJEA), a professional community built to support DJs who care about elevated standards, ethical sales, and long-term business health. His role is to be the guide, curating best practices, creating clarity, and helping DJs rise above the noise of low-price competition.

At the center of all his work is a simple belief:

How DJs are seen will always determine what DJs are worth.

This book gives you the tools to change that perception, starting with your very next conversation and advancing a larger mission to strengthen the industry together.

CLIENTS SPEAK ABOUT DJEA RESOURCES

"My name is Mark Brenneisen, the president of Total Entertainment in Hudson Falls, New York. Before DJ's Edge, our business looked like everybody else's business in the area. Our ads looked the same. Our waste of time was the same. And, I mean, we were good, but we just didn't have that professional edge that Mark's program really helped us with.

Since DJ's Edge, our business increased 200% easily, and we've only really been one full year in this program. It happened very quickly and very easily because we cut our sales time down; we weren't wasting time anymore with those long consultations on the phone. And it was always a hassle to get those "How much do you charge for this type of event?"on the phone people into the office. Once they're here, they're ours.

If you're considering using the DJ's Edge program, and you haven't done it yet, you're an idiot. It's one of the most effective tools in our industry that you can have because there are so many different secrets. Mark and his team have put this to-gether. It's probably the best investment you'll ever make. The flyer that Mark mailed to us sat there for three months, but I didn't throw it away, because I was like, 'Man, this sounds way too good to be true.' So finally, I took the time, and I started calling around to some of Mark's clients and DJs, and the first thing out of all their mouths was, 'Before we go any further, don't waste time, just buy it.' I was like, 'Well, answer my questions first.' I spoke to three guys across the country, all of whom told me I had already waited too long to buy it. So they answered all my questions and gave me all the information. And finally, when I spoke to Mark's team, they answered more questions. And we made the investment, which just returned itself in a few short months, and it did everything Mark said it would. And I think the biggest thing was Mark giving us permission to use his format.

When we used that format, it did exactly what the program said it would. It cut our sales time down to nothing. There was no more sitting on the phone with people for an hour. It was like five minutes, get their information, bang it out, and that was it. We mailed them the package. And next thing you know, we probably have about an 85% rate of people calling back, making that first consultation, coming into our office, and once they're here, there's probably also around an 85% to 90% rate of them giving us a retainer. And so that's where we finally bought it, and from then on, everything Mark said was right on. It was ridiculous, Paul and I, my manager, were laughing while listening to the CDs. We realized that we never knew how to sell ourselves. We just talked over the phone, but when we got Mark's program, everything changed for us."

Mark Brenneisen
Total Entertainment
Hudson Falls, NY

$\sim$

"My name is Alex Morales, from Prime Time Music Entertainment, and I'm from Chino, California. I've learned that marketing and sales are the keys to success in our business, and it's just unbelievable how important they are. I always thought it was about the equipment and how good my mixing skills were. I never realized how important marketing and sales were.

I also learned to have the confidence to actually raise my rates. And that was another important thing, especially since I'm a full-time DJ, and that was vital for me to be successful. It's kept me away from going back to a nine-to-five job. I'm 34, and when I bought the system, I already had a 1-year-old. My wife was expecting the second baby, and I really had to make changes. I had to make some real money and increase my bottom line. Mark's system is too good to be true. It's priceless. It has absolutely changed my DJ life and the way I think about how the business runs. I wish I had picked up the system 5 or 10 years ago, to say the least. But it is priceless."

Alex Morales
Prime Time Music Entertainment
Chino, CA

∽

"After 14 years in DJ entertainment, Mark Imperial's DJ industry-specific coaching supercharged our business. We expanded into events and rentals, landing a $5,400 multi-day booking, and I hadn't even finished Mark's program yet—proving every penny invested returns in multiples. Wives of DJ owners: Don't fear the leap; gain the knowledge and watch your growth soar!"

Gabriel & Margarita Lara
JSP Entertainment
San Antonio, TX

∽

"This is Doug Gazlay. I'm a DJ in Atlanta, Georgia. I think that you can definitely just keep doing this the way you're doing it. I would definitely refer your system, Mark, to anyone working in the DJ market who is trying to organize their mind, because we have a lot of ideas as creative DJs. Creativity

does not always organize well. And you really helped me focus, which is why I would refer anyone to you. I think you've put together, in a clear way, how we can streamline the things we need to do to make our businesses successful. So thank you once again, my friend. I'm glad to be part of the inner circle and wish all the best to everyone."

Doug Gazlay
Atlanta, GA

~

"Hi, everybody at DJ's Edge,

Booked my first gig off the videos you made. The couple didn't even have to meet with me because you made me look so good here in Scottsdale, Arizona.

As you promised, I'm making my competition crazy. Keep up the good work!"

Eric Chudzik
Electric Blue Entertainment

www.ingramcontent.com/pod-product-compliance
Lightning Source LLC
Chambersburg PA
CBHW060333050426
42449CB00011B/2746